From Time-Buried Years

David Norris-Kay

Indigo Dreams Publishing

Second Edition, From Time-Buried Years
First published in Great Britain 2009

Indigo Dreams Publishing
24 Forest Houses
Cookworthy Moor
Halwill
Beaworthy
EX21 5UU

www.indigodreams.co.uk

David Norris-Kay has asserted his right under the Copyright, Designs
and Patent Act 1988 to be identified as the author of this work.
davidnorriskay@gmail.com

©2009 David Norris-Kay
©2014 Twelve additional poems

ISBN 978-0-9553589-7-5

British Library Cataloguing in Publication Data. A CIP record for this
book can be obtained from the British Library.

Designed and typeset in Times New Roman by Indigo Dreams

Printed and bound in Great Britain by Imprint Academic, Exeter.

Cover design by Ronnie Goodyer at Indigo Dreams

Dedication

To the memory of my parents, Joyce and Douglas –

They would have been proud.

Also to the servicemen and women who gave their lives for our

freedom in two world wars. – Lest we forget.

By The Same Author:

The Moss Garden 2003
A Beggars' Feast 2004
Vanishing Sun 2007

(This book is a collation of new work and selected poems from my previous publications)

Acknowledgements

I would like to thank my fellow poets for their help and support:
Harry Crompton-fils, Margaret Whitaker, Albert Oxford, Barbara Robinson, June White, Mary Stringer, Brian Smith, and, most important, Ronnie Goodyer for bringing this book into being.
I was very grateful for the encouragement of the late poets George Kerridge and Margaret Munro Gibson and I express my enduring appreciation to their families in fond memory of them.

I am also indebted to the following, who have accepted, or previously published, some of the work within these covers.

SALOPEOT (The Salopian Poetry Society), ISTHMUS (Ouse Valley Poetry), INCLEMENT MAGAZINE, ATLANTEAN PUBLISHING, CANDELABRUM, REACH POETRY, CARILLON MAGAZINE, COUNTRYSIDE TALES, THE POETIC CIRCLE OF FRIENDSHIP, METVERSE MUSE (India), FORWARD PRESS, PAUSE, FREEXPRESSION MAGAZINE (Australia) and THE NATIONAL POETRY ANTHOLOGY (UNITED PRESS)

FOREWORD

Within this sensitively presented tapestry of abiding recollection, those long-treasured moments of a perceptive poet/writer's yesterday's world are so vividly represented in what has effectively become the very definitive collection of his major poetic endeavours.

Sheffield-based poet, David Norris-Kay, has for many years been achieving far-reaching (and several times prize-winning) acclaim throughout the well-subscribed circuit of small-press poetry magazines, and it is here, within this worthy collection , 'FROM TIME-BURIED YEARS' (now into its second edition) that a number of these previously published poems have been so lovingly brought together.

Despite this modest poet's assertions to the contrary, it is decidedly apparent that David is a versifier of extensive accomplishment, with noticeable leanings towards the traditional genre, as his fine included sonnets, villanelles and well-ordered quatrains readily reveal. The timeless quality of his work, brilliant in portrayal, and abounding in assonant and alliterative detail, is sensuously imbued with poignant memories of childhood days, and an openness of love for those close to him who had ever been so vital to his day-to-day existence.

Lyrical in quality, and pleasingly eloquent in word and phrase, this is a collection that just had to be written, so that those drifting TIME-BURIED YEARS may, in this fitting way, be given the lasting perpetuity that they so richly deserve.

Bernard M. Jackson
International Review Writer

The additional twelve poems were chosen by friends and followers as personal favourites they would like to see included in this book.

David Norris Kay

CONTENTS

From Time-Buried Years

David Norris-Kay

CHILDHOOD HOME

I stood in a grip of ice
That froze and tossed these old walls
In a tumble of time.
This now-roofless shell,
Which once cradled my
Incipient warmth,
Wrapped my formative years
In a strong embrace
Of sun-stretched days,
And moon-mingled nights
Where quick cats darted through
The garden's sleeping flowers.

Magical summers sang
Their high notes
Through crowded raspberry canes,
And blown poppies blushed
Where dancing emerald blades of grass,
Tickled my freshly formed feet
In whispers of fluting air.

Glancing on my early bed,
A lone, bright star
Set in window glass
Shone faintly on my face
As I painted mind-pictures
From wallpaper patterns,
And watched
Far away house lights
Ripple with curtained thoughts.

Crackling smoky autumn fires:
Sledges sliding lamp-lit tracks
In the cream of winter snows,
Curl back on a tide of years
To soak the cold, empty shell
In happy life once more:
And this sudden rush of memory
Brings my singing childhood home.

SONNET: THE CRAFT

Sweet words my mother taught me have now grown,
And opened up like flowers on a hill,
Their shoots have multiplied, their seeds far-blown
On winds of change that stir creation's will,
And from my inspiration's seething fire,
A cauldron of emotions are conceived
Which boil and mix hard ice with hot desire,
Until a thread of meaning is retrieved.
This thread is twisted, woven, then composed;
Moulded into neat traditional form,
Soon wells of fire are capped and tightly closed,
Where logic overpowers raging storm.

　　　The writer's craft, aspiring into art,
　　　Combines both fire and ice within my heart.

BUTTERFLY

There is no savagery or ruthless vice
In this unchained flower,
Dragon-flamed wings ignited
By the snaking-grasses fuse.

Mantras of war are for birds, beasts and men
To chant incessantly
Until they draw
Their last rattling battle-breath:

You rise from the killing-grounds
To celebrate the sun,
A nectar-primed power-pack
Crackling with the potency of flight:

Flashing over a tree-bordered twilight of water,
Born with the weed-seed
On singing sedge-combed breezes
Which stir the haystack's flaxen thatch:

You are an aeolian ghost:
Brought on a wind of dreams from lost childhood,
Red admiral of blushing skies
Haunting sorrel-sown spinneys of summer:

Evoking from time-buried years,
A laughing, bright-eyed innocence, which drove
My agile body through swaying wheatfield dawns
Dense with the kindling colours of quivering wings.

I caught you clinging to a bending poppy's plume,
Like a fragment of the setting sun,
Ephemeral as smoke, yet graceful in your dying,
Bowing out to the cloud-crinkled evening.

(First prize winner in the Salopian Open Poetry Competition 1981)

COTTON-TOP

Hair blowing blonde
like cotton grass,
I was you
as you blossomed
through tempestuous time,
reached for wide horizons
stretching from the door
through which you crawled
on chubby knees.

You hid
in your under-table haven
as I looked through your eyes
at new, amazing worlds
throwing shadows
and dancing highlights
on endless possibilities,
that slanted through rain, sunshine
and spiralling snows.

Adult heads bent,
cooed, "Isn't *she* sweet."
Beneath the pram-shade
I slept unaware,
in the innocence of my rising
song. Destined
for bearded poethood
when the rushing years
had streamed beyond my harbour..

Oh angel-pop, oh cotton-top,
you remain within the man.

STORM, AND I (aged 6)

Slabs of cloud built up a heaven,
and I dreamt in it. I tottered
on a wooden seat: garden bench,

weathered, twisted by rain and sun.
Granddad carefully wrought it with
wizened hands on his lathe of years.

My fists flayed in fragrant air's warmth,
steaming from scattered, studded cups
of late tulips, their heads breeze-bent

against a vibrancy of sky
stacked slab upon slab, black and grey
atmospheres in a swirling dome.

Inflated fear suddenly burst
into a force of heat, and drove
the high energy of my leap

from weathered wood into a drift
of petals in the grasses draught,
where I rolled in hip-tickling fronds,

hay-smell comforting, knees scraping
on the rooted ground, and strange skies
turning and turning my vision's

dizzy motion to the cracked clouds
which thundered like hammers on tin
as the bench tipped onto harebells

by my bare legs, and the black storm
hovered like an angry eagle
in wild spaces of the sky's reach:

sudden calm shivered leaden light.
I rose from gaunt grass, a surprised
witness to the unstable stars.

FALLING

Close your eyelids
Onto warm darkness,
Where sun-mists diffuse
The sky's bright lens:
Holding your image
In faultless beauty,
As you fall
Into the timeless
                        dream
Of infancy.

FATHER
(In fond memory of Douglas Norris)

Always assured and strong, he held me,
Six feet high, to clip the hedge with toy shears;
Tickled me in blowing summer grasses;
Picked ripening raspberries; red juices
Staining hands and lips, as the soft sun sank
Through banked purple clouds of evening's glory.

His large hands plucked me through falling twilight:
Perched on broad shoulders, I rode through orchards:
Leaves brushed my blushing cheeks with cooling green,
As his boots crushed fallen fruit and king-cups,
Cut fragrant paths through densely woven shoots
Beneath faint constellation's sparkling glow –

I still remember those blossoming stars
Blazing in domed night above the dark house,
As he related tales of lost childhood
His voice fading as my heavy eyelids
Closed, and a fire of dreams lit the blackness
In a deep, soothing symphony of sleep.

I saw his safe and solid form emerge
From a packed, long awaited, rattling tram:
I shouted "Daddy", leapt into his arms,
Was gently carried to a fresh cooked tea;
Afterwards in the garden, we popped peas
From home-grown pods into a bowl of hope.

He steadied me throughout the turning years:
The ever-pouring, rushing stream of time,
But couldn't quite prepare me for the jolt
Of his demise before three score and ten,
Although his laughter, strength, and moral ways,
Steady me still, - through solitary days.

MOTHER

Enfolding lavender apron:
Arms bearing warm gifts of comfort
To embrace her child of the sun.

She wrapped me in an innocence
Which endured down her grinding life's
Pain pitted pathways, to an end

Even her piously believed
Gods could not see: oblivion
Awaiting the headlong motion

Towards a selfless enigma.
She endures in my body still:
A gushing fountain in my veins

Carries the pulse of her being,
Bringing a sad nostalgia
To haunt her legacy of years…

Whose kindness desiccates its tears.

WASHING

Bed sheets cut out squares of sky,
White as virgin's frocks: Mother's
Water-wrinkled hands pegged them

On quivering, wind-plucked lines,
Drawn taut as violin strings.
Her child skips in the sun's grasp.

Ancient washboard's hard knurled kiss,
Left leavings of laundered sheets,
Plaited: wrung dry as a cough,

Ready to hang in blown air;
Fascinating her girl's gaze.
Their slow, hypnotic billows

In steep sky's deep bowl, ripple
Like fluttering flags of truce,
Raised up to the work-cracked day.

Sweet daughter lies prone. Beneath
The strung sheet's ballooning heave:
Suddenly leaps up, happy

As a lamb's giddy gambol,
Washing dreams with purity:
Standing on the brink of years.

(Third prize winner in The Salopian Open Poetry Competition 2005)

AFTERNOONS
(For Thomas, in memoriam)

Glancing sunlight paints memory's pictures
on afternoon's palette. Old photographs
stain with sepia my mind's probing thoughts
of Grandfather's 'almost forgotten' war:
his medal: "For bravery in the field" –
won for 'taking out' an enemy gun:
he crept mud-slow, sly, bayonet-ready,
at intervals faking death: did his job
to save men's lives. My room's unreal silence
holds dust-drawn sunbeams. An English stillness
returns me from rattling-rip of gun-storm
and despairing screams. Beyond lace curtains
a bird calls from high swaying summer trees.
I hear echoes of laughter from children
who are unaware. Wars that won this peace
are hidden beyond their horizon's grasp,
they don't really care. I say a prayer
for those lost men, who in the name of right
restored my peaceful sun-washed afternoons,
crushed invading hordes, and brought back the light.

BROTHERS-IN-WAR
(In memory of Harold and Don)

I didn't understand,
when I saw Grandmother's tears
splash onto the roses:
her busy trowel paused,
in the warm summer garden
of my childhood,

or when Mother gazed wistfully
at a faded photograph
of a uniformed man
leaning jauntily against a truck,
staring nonchalantly
into a non-existent future.

Now I know
that these moments of sadness
held the horrors of war:
sudden oblivion by gunfire
in the Somme's stinking mud.
Searing Egypt's shuddering tanks

and a shrieking-shrapnel waste
where the dead were piled
high as sandbags.
Men who never knew
the peace of roses;
were harvested by lancing lead...

Most didn't live to 'fight another day':
so-still they lay, soldiers Norris and Kay.

BETRAYAL

Night shook its stars across the window,
Oppressive as silence
that whispered with the child's plea:
"No more" – over and over.
Curling tight round her teddy bear
she trembled the time away,

till dreaded, heavy footfalls
thumped, crashed slowly upward…
Her door groaned open, spilled light,
and a shadow loomed, big as panic.
Its heavy bulk crushed down,
then breathless, spoke: "Be quiet now"…

Hot tears stormed over and over
where the pink duvet mocked
and nursery wallpaper stared blankly,
impotently, as if at a dark play.
Night shook its stars across the window,
and her silence screamed and screamed.

ANGEL (Children's Poem)

Rolling down bright banks of daisies,
bare-legs kicking in the air;
giggling with the joy of being,
sunshine lights her flaxen hair.

Skipping through the swaying meadow,
and buttercup's caress,
she laughs at golden glancing rays
that play upon her dress.

'How swift the purple evening falls:
its shadows safely keep
her gently cradled in the arms
of softly-dreaming sleep'.

(With help from Harry Crompton-fils)

THE INMATE

Trapped in a white room: fading flowers
Wilt in a plastic vase.
She stares through these fellow exiles
From a world of renewal and growth,
Out of the barred window
At a burgeoning elm:
Her only means of measuring time
As the years perform their slow
Monotonous dance.
She has watched a million elm leaves
Fall and crumble into death,
Envious of their dignity.
Each morning finds her more confused
In the clamour of the mental hospital:
A cold efficient machine
Running into eternity.
Her sobs echo from the faceless walls
Of the white room.
Ignored by starched-coated ghosts
Who haunt the sterile corridors,
She incessantly curses the system,
Which in ignorance long ago,
Committed her life to misery,
For bearing an illegitimate child.

SONNET: ROSES

(In memory of fellow poet Margaret Munro Gibson)

Where tumbled tors shadowed a stone-walled field,
And hostile aircraft skimmed encircling skies,
You showed determination not to yield,
To enemies of reason and their lies –
Like thorny briars creeping all around,
That pricked your conscience with a sterner view
Of England in her peril, then you found,
A clearer way where storm clouds broke anew:
Sudden shafts of sunshine warmed the briar,
And inspiration slowly came to bloom,
You found yourself within a softer shire,
Where peace, at last suffused a restful room,

> Your words, like roses blossomed from past strife,
> Composing verses of a worthwhile life.

(Margaret served her country as a height finder for heavy anti aircraft guns (Ack Ack) in 1942)

DOLL

Abandoned in the swaying grass,
That blows beside a narrow lane,
Where pacing people seldom pass;
She lies exposed to drifting rain.

Forlorn beneath the circling skies,
A hidden hollow hides her form:
Soft raindrops are the tears she cries,
Sprayed from the remnants of a storm.

Where are the loving arms that held,
Her flaxen head in fond embrace?
The cherished gaze unparalleled,
Persisting from a faultless face –

The sweet face of a perfect child,
Who sheltered her in clasping hands;
A little girl yet undefiled;
She skipped through softly shifting sands.

The sands of time then slowly yield:
She fell headlong into its whirl:
The fresh growth of a summer field,
Is stunted by the winter's pearl.

Her cheeks now like a wrinkled prune,
And innocence defiled near death,
The child who long since passed her noon,
Is old and worn with laboured breath.

The doll still has a youthful bloom,
Although the child succumbed to time,
And still glows in the grasses' gloom
In summer warmth and winter rime.

SNOWDROPS

Beneath the leaf-green shadows, glow,
Pale buds that herald spring:
On borders of receding snow
Where grasping grasses cling.

Evoking early childhood days,
When I would lie for hours,
And see the slanting sunbeams blaze
Golden in the flowers.

Their faultless, sturdy blooms withstand,
The turbulence of skies,
And in the vernal warmth expand
To form wide bell-shaped eyes.

They watched my boyhood blossom bright
In simple innocence;
The swaying flowers lambent-white
With drooping indolence.

Now fading with the failing light,
Where spreads the dusk's calm haze:
The trembling petals closing tight,
Reflect the moon's faint rays.

WINTER 1975

Dry-stone walls cemented with snow,
Do not create boundaries
For the wet-layered white-silence
Falling from a leaden dusk...
Like a memory of the ice-age
Resurrected by the whining wind.

The world has shrunk
Into the compass of a Mammoth's eye:
The long bite of cold
Has penetrated deep into flesh:
I am a wounded animal, instinct-driven
Over a shrunken planet of pain.

Unaware that the sentinel-trees,
Half consumed by mist,
Sense in their root's buried darkness,
A furnace at the earth's core,
Inducing in the soil's warm womb
The first amniotic rush of spring.

BIRTH SONNET

Dark membranes tremble: slowly slide apart,
Revealing liquid amniotic gloom,
Distant sounds faded by a drumming heart,
Echoing spasms of a fruitful womb:
Dim daylight beckons beyond pulsing pain,
Promising things I cannot understand,
Like flowing rivers, and soft falling rain:
Far-reaching skies over emerald land.
Contractions quaking in my tender ears,
I uncurl quickly, pushed towards the light,
Driven by incipient, feral fears:
Commence the struggle of my mortal fight.

Emerging from Mother's darkness, I bring,
Fresh life to the dominion of spring.

SWAN

White ghost glides on the darkened mere,
With graceful neck coiled into space,
In peace that knows no inward fear,
She leaves a wake of laughing lace.

In rolling ripple's dancing moon,
A cygnet seeks her preening queen,
Who wakes a sylvan-piper's tune
That floats through glades of living green.

The slow span of her spreading wings,
Flings splashing stars on seas of night:
And where their breeze-borne echo rings,
The spectral swan will pass from sight.

*(First prize in the September heats of The Coast To Coast International Writing
Competition 2007 and third prize in the finals.)*

MOUSE

Incited by instinctive need
Yet held within a wooden jail,
Domesticated but still wild,
She turns a treadmill of dull days,
A living plaything for a child:
Small toy to tease and pertly pet,
Let out to briefly grace the grass,
Taste freedom from a fettered brain,
Before being cramped inside the cage
Where pangs of hunger tinge her pain.
She gnaws a block to burnish teeth
In preparation for the grain
The child will offer twice a day,
And nibble sundered from the sun...
This then: the sum of aimless life,
A year at most the torment trails
In the winding wake of waning,
Before I hold her gently cupped
And feel the failing feeble flesh
Of the furry body fading.

MOTH

Folded wings,
Veined as marble,
Are like a black
Pythagorean triangle:
A ship's sail's
Sunset silhouette
Against the bright glare
Of the lamp.

Aimless circled wanderings
On the shade,
Are perhaps a quest for freedom
From the attraction of light:

Like my quest
To escape temptation,
My blind adventures
In life's ravelled maze.

Take flight moth
Beyond the window,
Glee-driven wings
Dusted with hope:
Midnight's unsung freedom
Awaits.

I will follow this example
Of graceful escape,
Will leave the confines
Of my weaknesses.

Dormant adrenaline awakes,
Eager youth,
Victim of gradual
Submission to time –
Returns.

(Third prize winner in The Salopian Open Poetry Competition 1984)

ALDEBARAN
(Cinquain sequence)

Cold space:
star seething red
beyond the reach of man.
Child of nebulous Hyades,
now grown.

Your light
ignited when
Taurus bellowed its birth
to a universe of fire-pricked
darkness.

What worlds
of strange creatures
are held in your orbits?
What love and war are theirs to play
with fate?

Faint ghosts
blink in lenses:
spectres of light, long-dimmed,
dance in cold eyes of telescopes,
and mock

Our dream's
ongoing quest
to find companions
in a vastness of expanding
cosmos...

Now deemed
impossible,
like the resurrection
of our time-lost plays in childhood
havens.

Far sun,
spill your secrets
like nectar onto Earth:
their presence may save us a long
journey.

SUMMER SOLSTICE

Orange furnace-dawn illumes the trefoil,
Leaves locked in light under a fern frond's coil:
sea sounds hollow notes in sand's golden grains,
Ebbing and sighing its whispered refrains –
Where thunderous breakers sizzle to foam,
Wide patterns of waves remind me of home,
And a bubbling cauldron of childhood dreams,
Boils over my rim and runs down in streams,
Flowing where horizons, grass-girdled, fly,
Flung in a circle beneath blue-brushed sky.
Time passes quickly, borne through blurring tears,
Welling in whirlpools of swift swirling years:
Barefoot I run, leaving bright boyhood days –
In high sun's heat of summer solstice haze.

CONSIDERING A LEAF
(For June White)

Evokes a filament of youth
where sunray paints a summer wood
with dappled patterns of the past
which never can be understood.

Too complex patterns, shadows black,
are laid along our serried fears,
and in this leaf I see them traced
like veins of lifeblood through the years.

Such shadowed fears make us alive,
and mixed with joy, life's anthems sing
that from each Autumn's sad decay
awakes a seed of certain spring.

THE MILL STREAM

Chuckling under dripping fronds of willow,
Eternal flux of water, glazing stone,
Beneath the slow roll of a rotting wheel,
Stream slides forth like silk to surreal skyline,
Where bright bubbles ride on racing ripples,
Exploding in the spray of a cascade:
Starkly iridescent, a sparkling teem,
Pouring through a flyblown swathe of summer –
And I pause to conjure contemplation:
Evoke a view of long lost tender years
That bowl me, headlong to oblivion,
And skim me like a pebble over time.
Now tumbled, broken millstones block the skies,
Which, blushed with dawn bleed into stagnant pools,
That fill deep hollows by the living stream,
And spill their stars among taut, twisted weed.
Hypnotic movement captivates my mind,
Soft swaying meadow: water's gliding glass,
Vibrate in mystic unity to form
A raft of thoughts that permeate my view –
And I pause to contemplate the millers:
Not one in a generation could grind
A grain as fine as nature's seed, that grows
The balanced system of leaf and flower,
Moon, stars, sun and rain: crystal patterned snows:
Now tumbled mill is colonised: the wild
Gradually reclaims all that she owns –
And I pause to contemplate nature's rush,
Then sink in the solitude of her hush.

DUSK

To slip into dusk
Is a tranquil move,
Day fades from faces
And night's black
Star-peppered fear
Is only promised.

Dark gaps of windows
Steal the sun:
Reflect it outward
From the mirror-town.
The last gleam dies,
And moles in wonder
Burrow deep
Under spring.

The half-light
Halves life's stress,
And a fire leaps
Deep in your moon-flecked face;

Passion returns...

The dusk is filled
With deep-dredged flame.

BEGGARS' FEAST

Swollen sun candescent in cloud
Gathering in the east,
Birdsong chorus echoing loud
Heralds a beggars' feast.

They drink sweet draughts of open air,
Consume the vibrant view:
Bright breeze-blown grasses grace their lair,
Shining with drenching dew.

Fresh fields of bending barley sway
Against far purple hills,
And fruits of nature coaxed from clay,
An aching hunger fills.

A perfect praedial repast,
For poor-man, bird and beast,
Who end their bleak bucolic fast,
And join the beggars' feast.

DANDELIONS

They blaze
In the strangling grasses' grip:
Pinnately lobed leaves,
Dew dropped
In dawn's first flush:
Bright medallions
Sun-struck, peppered pale
With blizzard-blossoms
Flung through dancing air
From high hawthorns.

This blanching
Is a premonition of fluffy flight
In the season's turning,
When gossamer parachutes,
Float in leaf-littered skies,
Letting go their burdens
Over seed-scattered fields,
And again, with vernal warmth,
Will blaze like small suns
In studded grass.

BIRDSONG

Filtering through the close-grown leaves
Of rustling breeze-blown bushes weaves
A piping song, which ghosts the dawn
With fluting on the sun-struck lawn.

Through mist-marred morning meadows, calls
Are echoed from old ivied walls:
The squabbling tree-held birds will keep
Our children from their realms of sleep:

Ignites an urgency to rise,
And skip beneath blue-arching skies,
Where creeping shadows softly spread,
Cast by the branches overhead.

Sweet birdsong soothes a sudden strife,
And brings the balance back to life,
Attenuates our growing fears:
Mellifluous to muted ears –

And when the silence of the night,
Stills birdsong till the morning light,
Impatience fills the void until
I hear again the choral trill!

CLEMATIS

They dazzle from a darkened wall,
Four-pointed stars reflecting light,
Then one by one frail petals fall,
And smudge with snow the perfumed night.

Pale flower-fragments stir and drift,
Ephemeral along the road,
Leaving leaves which tremble and lift,
Unburdened of their heavy load.

And now no more those starry blooms
Stud rustling leaves with glowing grace:
Instead a green-tinged darkness looms,
Casting shadows across my face:

Soft shadows of swift passing years,
Over flower-flushed fields will fly,
Confirming all my fleeting fears –
And like the clematis go I.

SEA TANKA

Scintillating seas
Are like corrugated gold
In the sun's last glance,
As dusk drizzles falling fog
Onto fulgent foam flecked waves.

BLADDERWRACK

Sea like corrugated iron
rusts in oblique-sun's glance;
pours into tidal pools
where strips of bladderwrack sway,
bending to the current's wind.

brown rubbery sacs
swell in brackish murk,
bounce off rock-clamped limpets
sharp as incisors.

Small flashes of fish
silver a seaweed gloom,
make bubble-clouds burst
their brief orbs: a glittering
of spark-showers in water night

whose darkness hides monsters.

Giant rubber-bands of weed
choke-off rare oxygen:
strangle a slime of squids
in the pebble's grind.

Buoyant bladders break a surface
dancing with stars,
and a muted moon's face reflects
like an inquisitive hag,
the ripples' wrinkled etching.

AUTUMN'S REFLECTION

(£250 prize winner in the Forward Press Top 100 Poets Competition)
The cold astronomy of night
Imprints the Autumn chill,
And in the gale a crying voice
Tells tales from overseas:
'The soldier's boots are clods of mud'
'And bayonets slash the moon'
'A starving child gropes for a hand
To guide him through the war'

And leaves in England drift like waves
From green and brown to gold,
Reflecting pain that memory hides
Within its prison walls,
And the government will always win
The losses of the world,
As a poor man fights with waning strength
To keep a wife and child.

Too many hearts of stone exist
In the morning of a dream,
And fail to sense outside themselves
The wide expanse of love.
As winter's shadow covers fields
In quiet lands of snow,
The beast of progress devastates
The root of all that's true.

And no one ever will return,
To journey paths of sun,
Where a wasteland lies beneath the stars
Over which my words are flung.

Like empty caves in which the lies
Of nations echo through,
The hollow years destroy the smiles
Of those who breathe anew.

VILLANELLE FOR A DOVE

Beating wings facile in the frosty air,
As snowy skies from far horizons loom,
A white dove rises from its winter lair.

Purity and beauty beyond compare,
Ghosting the borders of a tree-dark gloom,
Beating wings facile in the frosty air.

Symbol of peace that soothes a dark despair,
Where gnarled looped branches tremble and entomb,
A white dove rises from its winter lair.

Faint fading stars briefly blossom and flare,
Light softly shining in my winter room:
Beating wings facile in the frosty air.

Cold gauzy cloud dims a swollen moon's stare,
Mirrored in ice like a petrified bloom:
A white dove rises from its winter lair.

Earth in iron grip, the bent trees leaf-bare,
Roots snow-deep, and above their drifted womb –
Beating wings facile in the frosty air;
A white dove rises from its winter lair.

WINTER 1967

Sound of wind
Through hollow stem,
Is reminiscent
Of summer's laughter
Taken away slowly
By seasons of time:

Before the face of stone
Was cold:
Before insects crawled
Beneath their suffering –

Bringing sleep
To aimless life.

My window frames
A world of flailing snow;
Of dead bees
And fading memories
Of warmer lands,

Where I looked out
On interstellar spaces,
Knowing Earth was lost

In that soft blackness.

But hope is in the haze
Of winter's grace,
And, sure as a rebirth
Of green –

We shall be found,
And our exile
will
be
ended.

DISEASE

What is this sickness
That beats like slowing clockwork
Where my spirit wants to leap with life?
An unknown disease weakens and wastes me,
While the brash, external world
Flaunts its mocking strengths,
And children smile perfect summers
From their unconscious joy.

The clouds on my mind's horizons
Are grim, uncompromising hospitals,
Locking love and sentiment
Outside their secrets
Of frustration and death.

How many long winters
Will dip the trees into ice?
How many suns will fly
Like burning kites
Over playgrounds of innocence,
before my clockwork stops - -

And the seasons bowl on into eternity,
Holding their photographs of what is lost.

MUSIC

Who are we to perceive what things
Are in the music of the strings?
Guitars and synthesisers sigh
Of variations in one sky.

So when the madness grows intense,
The madness of experience,
We pull the shade of love to drown
The jangling music of the town

SUNRISE
(Greece 1983)

Night's crucible spills gold
Over shadowy Sithonia:
A silent, swollen sun
Heralds the rebirth
Of arcane seascapes,
Where happiness
Sings like the sirens,
And the drunken,
Vibrant light,
Ebbs and flows like love
In the flaxen hair
Of a child.

SANTORINI

Sun-held alleys of whitewashed stone –
Dark cliffs topped white as burnished bone,
Cubist dwellings reflecting light
Seem to sway on a dizzy height,
And depths of dream in sky's soft haze,
Unravel thoughts of halcyon days,
Where seabirds wheel beneath the sun:
On crumbling walls quick lizards run;
Now, like a hawk, descends the night,
And foam-flecked waves fade out of sight:
Where countless galaxies above
Are mirrored in a sea of love:
From Delphi fair Apollo flies,
Gives back to men their youthful eyes –
To scan the whole horizon's arc
For stars like holes in velvet dark,
And where volcanic beaches lie,
Beneath a moon about to die,
Small twinkling towns wedged into night
Are luminous with spectral light;
Their ghostly glow pervades blue domes,
Whose crosses protect human homes:
The moon-held alley's soft-lit stone
Hems me in lamplight, all alone.

(Third prize winner in The Coast to Coast International Writing Competition 2005)

HOME FROM GREECE

Bright vacationer lands regress to dream,
When dark rain asserts its despondent hold,
Returning to a claustrophobic scene,
An unwilling 'black sheep' enters the fold.

My aspirations reached their finest hour
In air nebulous with incessant sun,
But now ambition's wraith, repressed and sour,
Lies fetid in a vacuum bled of fun.

Don't ask me in my present cold remorse,
What dreams I realised in those foreign nights:
I danced with strangers, rode a Greek's black horse:
Played the satyr in dionysic rites.

My dreaded anathema is the pain
Of stepping down from heaven's heady heights,
To fasten inhibition's heavy chain
With reason's lock around taboo delights.

VILLANELLE: MY ENGLAND

In this changed country that I once held dear,
Our selfish, crass ambitions gain control:
I wish the people would be more sincere.

If only folk would sometimes shed a tear,
Instead of being cold within their soul,
In this changed country that I once held dear.

Life's problems are like rocks that rise too sheer,
And getting over them can take its toll:
I wish the people would be more sincere.

Our future days now seem devoid of cheer,
And doubts obscure a strived-for moral goal,
In this changed country that I once held dear.

I hope we can in future quell the fear
That over our existence slowly stole:
I wish the people would be more sincere.

Dark forces in my England then should clear,
Returning to the values that console,
In this changed country that I once held dear,
I wish the people would be more sincere.

STANAGE SUNSET

I hang fire –

Watch secret valleys
Blink into being,
And conflagrations
Of spider trees
Fill shadow with sparks.

Sky is a skeleton
With a ribcage-furnace
Casting dreamscapes
In feathered bones –

I turn blinded
To a black cool of stone,
Sharp silhouettes sway
On the fire's rim:

Air heavy with rainbows
Sings in a gulley's flute,
Land softens into a dream:

I crunch for home.

RAVENSDALE

In Derbyshire's most secret heart,
Where wild colours burn into wild skies
Through the dark nets of trees,
And distant suns blaze like neon baubles
Beyond the translucent window of night,
My youth, like a fragile egg,
Was pillowed by winds and grasses
Against the pillaging sins of man.

My heart beat with insect's wings,
Pulsed with soft birdsong;
Longed to be impaled by peace –
To the beauty,
In this verdant cleft of suspended time,
Until earth is burnt in its own star's end,
And a cool blanket of space
Swathes my soul in oblivion.

When my lips
Are sealed forever against my hungers,
When my loved ones' cataclysmic tears
Fail to melt my mask of death:
Claim me Ravensdale,
Hold my spirit
In your pulsing power of peace,
My joyous womb of youth.

NEAR HATHERSAGE
(Derbyshire)

Summer has grown long in the weed.
Trees loop a cracked lane
With mad-entwining foliage,
Fragrant and forever dusk:
Dense domain of bees.

Soft, then wildly dark,
The landscape matches clouds,
Whose transient vapours
Blossom like slow explosions
In blue-arching-deeps of sky.

Squat, like a stone lion
On the patch-worked meadows,
North Lees Hall,
Thornfield of the Brontes,
Sleeps in history's sober shadow.

Through dream-misted eyes
I see the spectres
Of Jane Eyre and little Adèle
Cloud old windows with emotion
Fixed in fiction's timeless world.

Darkness falls: bringer of mystery;
Lost love's memory fills me with tears
Which fall like ice-beads
To the leaf-mould earth:

But joy soars in the night breeze,
Seeps from the hall's shadowed stones,
Bringing smiles from a past
Cradled in love.

Love that will return to me,
As to all who seek peace
And respite from an urban chaos.

CONCRETE CITY LOVE

Constructions fashioned by man's hand,
Rise tall upon a once-green land,
No idle dream: but what was planned;
And while each cold concrete tower
Tells man that man still thinks what's sour,
We stand firm possessed with power
Of love where love sustains each hour

STRANGE CITIES
(For Adèle)

Sailing into strange cities
From the open sea,
In the night the foreign ship
Sailed away from me:

I thought of you
As a lonely star,
High in the night
Of the world:
I pined for you
Not only then,
But round the lighted dial
Of time.

I'm sailing by
The winds of time.

Circling down on strange cities
From the open sky,
Alien towers in the sunshine
Gently falling by:

I wanted you
Like a silver bird
Wants the lift of the wind:
I smiled for you
Like you used to smile
When seeing me again:

I'm gliding on
The wings of time,
Searching for my dreams.

(Placed in The Inclement Poetry Competition 2004)

SUNDAY

Among those clustered
Grey blocks,
Which pass
As houses,

The magic
Of a glance,
Reunites the Sabbath
With love,

Joining
The frayed ends of certainty
Within our relief.

For are we not
In bondage?

Lovers
By the ghost legion of memory.

The marked trace
Through history
Of similar Sunday
                    Glances.

FIRE

Love is a shadow
That falls over thought.
Fills cold hearts with fire,
Where reason flounders,
Destroyed by her sparks.

Two furnace-fused minds,
Welded, locked in a
Synthesis. The fast
Flight of passion's pace
Tempts oblivion.

I'm enslaved by pure
Liberating flames
Burning inside her;
Shot with silhouettes
Of drunken desire.

Keep me imprisoned
In her shadow's kiss.
A sunburst of dreams
Feeds my driven dawns:
Fires her soft shadow.

THE FORGOTTEN VIRGIN

I found a depth in a Renoir...
Unlike the gallery
The painting lived.

And I drew from your nearness
Something similar
But not as void
As this now distant portrait:

A depth not measured but travelled
By unyielding,
Un-superficial affection

Flowing outward and blending
With a depth which flows outward
From my eyes.

We were lost in a fused space
Unknowing of the portrait's
Forgotten virgin...

But now I walk lonely
And stare.

GIRL IN THE TREES

Face set in green
Ease me from darkness,
My limbs thrash
And drown in men's
Mute savagery.

Shy eyes in leaves,
Moon-pale skin
Ghosting mists,
Fill me with lost diamonds
Flashing from a deep dawn.

You are a fading photograph
Scattered with dust –
Remote winds
Turning your corners –
Fragile and lost
In the brown thrusting power
Of living wood:
You have left me alone –

Your image blurs

In tear-stained eyes.

PORTRAIT

Falsely romanticised
By the camera's eye,
You gaze into the furnace
Of your bright world –
Watching my love
Burn in your disregard
For attachment.

Girl your beauty fills
The fissures of my brain,
Till only your image remains
In the wreck of life,
Like a flower
In the dark of insanity,
Where no smiles are...

And after all

You merely glance
At my passing shadow.

POEM FROM A ROOM (1971)

Shadows deepen the room-
And the city's darkness is a vague dream,
Sinking in silences of sleep:
Our sleep,
Beneath heavy eyes.

Upon the ceiling's cracked facade,
Neon movies of a lost summer
Seem to flicker with the passing lights
Of every solitary car -
Bringing a new and premature warmth
To the cold clouds of gloom
Hanging patiently over our smiles.

For there's nothing so simple as love,
Or so complicated as what it may bring,
And laughter is the only shield
We hold against our conflicts.

The cars have left the road outside,
Which the Romans built when conquering,
And in the silence we laugh -
And make love.

(Appeared in The National Poetry Anthology 2008)

MORNING

I greet the morning
As a barrier,
Not a grey adventure:
As I should.

Having sailed the night on dreams,
Waking frequently to delay time
With gaps in sleep.
Trying to reject the remorse
Pleasure leaves in passing;
Without success.

A storm of imagination
Troubles the hills and valleys
Of your body:
Thought explores light
And seeks further escape
In amorous journeys....

Outside the traffic awakes:
A dreary exodus begins.
I must join this queue
Of fog-born lumbering shapes,
Take my part
In an English city's ritual.

The puddles are mirrors.
In them can be seen
Last night's rain....
And hope.

LEGACY
(For Adèle – to be read 'Afterwards')

Now I am dead...

Your silent room becomes pervious
To torrents of memory:
My diaries and books
Lying open on the floor,
And consumed by the flames
Of your lingering love,
Embroider your thoughts
With the private tapestries we wove as one,
Before the years buried me
In their sediments of time.
You are conscious only
Of your limbs which held me:
Your lips and moist eyes
Which cooled my fevers and fears
In the bubbling wake of our happiness.

I still smile for you
Though I drift
On planes unconnected to the mortal world.
Enjoy the ghosts of laughter I have left behind
On our holy fields of flowers,
Where now a strange landscape of modern steel
Extends its boundaries into darkness:
For memories, unknown to you-
Are realities, eternally set
In incomprehensible domains,
Where past, present and future co-exist.

My immortal eyes
Encompass your agony of separation:
See you crouched at the window
Which only permits a view of your empty present:
Past and future
Seem like shadows cast by your sighs for me,
Diaphanous visions, like mute marionettes
Jerked on the spectral-strings of your consciousness.
Patience, my love,
I too wistfully watch and wait,
Sundered, until you join me

Leaving your empty shell,
A gift for the barren ground.

SONNET: LOSS
(For Gilly)

Now evening ends the golden day at last,
and spans of sunlight turn to indigo.
Pale ghosts of people conjured from the past
file silently through summer's afterglow,
where sadness and regret in stark relief
are cast like shadows on the paths I took:
The ways which led through my entrenched belief
that hope would grow from every kindly look.
Oh frigid fate that turned life's hopes around,
and vanquished them as sure as daylight dies,
has robbed me of each hard won piece of ground,
and dimmed the light of beauty in my eyes:

no people left to pacify my pain:
my poems the only gift that will remain.

SPACES

I am a space between spaces:
Between summit and sky:
Clough and clouds,
I am an enigma: The fulcrum
Of shadow and light –
Where love has turned full circle
From youth's primeval song
Of moor and rock
Through the arcane worship
Of woman and child,
To the present hiatus:
Where open spaces evoke,
Like summer flowers,
The light of a million
Tranquil dreams.

TIME FLIES

Driven by the taut spring of youth
I feel immortal,
Inviting childish laughter
Into my ignorance of old age.

Sapling-supple bones
Arrayed in summer flesh,
Move in a celebration
Of lively warmth.

Unheeded,
A winter hatches in the marrow:
Spreads unhurried disorder
Through green age:

Too soon the joy of my body
Will be ash,
Bricked in a wall of remembrance,
Which will easily be forgotten.

CHILD

When sun's red disc fired cloud-strands of dawn,
And the playground was damp with dew,
I, fresh from dream, stretched young legs,
Raised wondrous eyes to vibrant heaven,
And gulped morning air like my first breath.

It was another beginning: fresh spray
Sprinkled cool flesh, seas thundered on breakers
In the moving sand. O how my body
Worshipped the breeze, and joy filled
A whole dome of sky.

I commanded the sighing foam: it was flux
Between my toes. Tingling feet kicked
A dazzle of droplets in sun streaked air,
They fell onto wavelets, rained
In my salt caked hair:
A shower of molten gold.

Then back to the playground; a swing's arc
carried me through cool blue. It was six years
Since birth. I was a silk-skinned traveller
In a new world; fresh fruit in a strange orchard
Of sensations.

I ran: legs flashing like seagull's wings
In sunlight. I flew over emerald grass, flowers
Shining in a green cosmos. bare feet
Treading galaxies of daisies. I was a meteor,
Chasing echoes of laughter
Through sparkling dominions.

Incipient power of growing stirred a storm;
Taut energy released. I was catapulted
Through environs of dreams, down a slide of days,
A multitude of dawns.
Fresh and pure, forever plunging
Into foam-curled waves:
Gliding with the high gulls –

And always, always the child.

SCARBOROUGH 1958

Men in hats and overcoats
black as a murder of crows,
trod their shadows beside
stout harbour walls. Rocking, bright
patterns of boats
bobbed brown water
and gulls screeched a white sky's echo
above fish-fleshed foam.

There, Mother led her boys
in a brave undress towards
the cold waves. Threading through
deck chairs and Father's lazy
trouser-rolled pose, their
water-slapped feet sank,
in soaked sand-swirl
and the pebbles hurt.

They swished, giggled till light failed
and lamps ignited a flicker
against turned-black sky:
Then bare-legged it
back to boarding house soup,
down light-threaded roads
redolent with fried fish,
and tomorrow's threat of home.

LONGING

(For the child within)

I hear in dreams
The whisper of leaves
From childhood summers,
Softly calling me to leave
This dissolute body-
And run once more,
Laughing and lissom
Among children,
Where loud birds
Shake the elms,
And morning
Bends through prisms
Of flower-held dew.

Time release me
from this prison,
Whose bars are bones
More stubborn than iron-
So I may seek beyond death
The sun-spangled trees,
Where I long to return
In the form of a child.

AUTUMN SECRETS
(From a 1986 Photograph)

The taller, younger girl -
Aged ten,
Whispers in the smaller,
Older girl's ear:
Both clutch Autumn-yellowed leaves,
Like portents of a future
Couched in disillusion.

A faded-green backcloth
Of diffuse trees
Adds a pastel sadness
To the contrast
Between young and decay,
Bringing a swell of tears
To my ageing eyes.

Their ageless ghosts
Have haunted me
Through crushing years.
Those vulnerable victims
Of circumstance
Run through a dream's span
Leaving echoes of laughter
Ringing through empty love.

I often wonder
What monstrosities they have become:
So painful to imagine them
Grown bulky and tired with time:
My thoughts
Hold two changeless children,
Forever whispering secrets
Of a lost Eden.

CROWD

Autumn has funnelled Summer
Into shivers.
Its vapours rise up, crowd
Into black, animal-shaped
Storm-heads:
Lions swollen with roars
Leap through cracks of thunder;
Pounce
On rain-needled dark,
Flickering with flashes.

Storm-startled, I cower
In the moor's
Wind-rumoured howlings.
Whipped with seething bracken,
I plunder deep valleys
For salvation: Expectations
Falter in crackling air,
And my nemesis
Advances in a crowd
Of deceptive, ancient Gods.

DEVOTION
(For Adéle)

What love the world cannot destroy
Is linked between our eyes?
What door leads to the garden
Where true devotion lies?

No greater understanding
Can lace our darkened years:
No mystery more eternal
Than love's abundance here.

Embracing all, in quiet words,
When first your shadow touched my heart,
And still remembrance here beheld
Of painful moments thrown apart.

And if fate's destiny is death,
Devotion still remains a whole,
Uniting love and life beyond,
Unbroken thought which binds the soul.

And when prayer fails to bring solace
From troubled words and jest,
I seek devotion harboured in
The hollow of your breast.

Unchanging in affection,
This love eternal lies,
In the shallow of our sunlight,
And deepness of our eyes.

(Appeared in 'Heart Shoots' (IDP) in aid of the Macmillan Cancer Charity)

DRAGONFLIES

Ghostly, Omni-directional,
Stirring micro-paths
Twisting through Summer's
Fragrant jungles of blossom:

Alighting weightless,
Spider-limbs quiver,
Beneath a fragile form
Reflecting
Morning glimmers
On hazy ponds
Of rippled light;

Delicate as sunshine:
Folding gossamer wings,
Under drooping fronds of willow.

Young girl reclines
In dappled shadow.
Hears a soft fluting
Of wind-song, drifting
Through tall reeds,
Directed
At the delicate insect –

Flitting darkly past her slender legs,
Like some fairy of herself;
Illuminated briefly
By Heaven's
Golden fire.

Two Dragonflies
In a birdsong morning.

ENDURANCE
(For Graham)

New scattered toys unwrapped the gloom
of winter days through frost-treed glass,
where brothers budding in the joy
of early years watched seasons pass.

A special bond exists, and more;
with sibling-love we lit the sun
and fired the sky-strung lantern-stars:
Shared fantasy contrived from fun.

Scattered toys in time have broken,
experience now long matured:
Still our bonding love as children
through consternation has endured.

FOG

Its moisture trembled
In beaded cobweb-tracery,
Spattered among leaves
In a long-ago garden.
Conceived from coal fires
And diffusing the solid into shade,
It drifted through a tundra
Of twigged clods.

Dimmed lamps flickered,
Guttering gaslight
On damp cobbles.
I rode a keen, high song
Of gauzy childhood,
In Mother-comforting
Warm-hearthed dreams
Fired in ember-glow.

The same white haze
Seeps into present time:
Blows through our dull
Decaying lives, held
In a noose of years:
Now turned grey as stone,
Fog filters into futures
Of retrospective ghosts.

HEARTHSIDE

Dreams are flickering in the flames:
Nostalgic images flash by,
of tricycles and swaying grass
from gardens where Spring swallows fly.

Bright glow evokes a childhood warmth,
that permeates the winter-grey,
and bolsters hope where hope had gone:
Now lights a smile to lift the day

from awkward ways of hopelessness,
and brings to mind those simple games
I used to play when time was green
and new dreams flickered in the flames.

HOUNDKIRK MOOR
(Yorkshire, England)

The frost has brought freshness: A new landscape
Spreads into a circle of horizons.
Grey lowering sky darkens, like a wedge
Driven by the wind into silences.

I take stock of black cracked rocks, balanced on
Sharp cloud-ridged edges: A ghost-balloon sun,
Diffused with fog like oppressive despair
Shivering the margins of tiredness..

There is a brotherhood here: A secret
Gathering of elements, welling up
In winter whitenesses over Cam Height –
A trudge away in a cauldron of storm.

Sky's swollen pregnancy of snow howls forth,
Thickens exposed roots into snagging knots.
My limbs protest in absolute zero:
I stagger over tussocks like a lush.

JOANNE

Encapsulated in her gaze
Pale Dreamy ghosts of fleeting years
Turn on a fulcrum forged from days
Which balance all our hopes and fears.

Such innocence and love are there,
Inside the unselfconscious blue
The permeates her steady stare,
And wakes all happy dreams anew.

Now skipping down sun's shadowed rays,
In dark and light of dappled years,
She smiles through all her joyful days
To lift me from depressive tears.

LORRAINE, AGED 8

A perfection of childhood
I never attained,
Shines from your eyes
Like Elysian fields
Of endless summer.

Weed trails gossamer-ice
Where you run and laugh,
Blonde and elusive
Across a gulf of years.

Soft face:
Fragment of sunshine,
Snares me in an aching
Exigency of love -

Clouds pale,

Feeling flows into voids
Like a liquid -

Drowning

Dissent that flares
On our borders.

I reach a hand....
To grasp your pure song
In the hidden dens of June:

My stain cannot taint
Your virtuous,
Visionary pools of light:

I become flotsam -
Born on a wave of blossom
As it crashes and dies
On my fading, adult shores.

(Gossamer-Ice: A metaphor for the fluffy seeding of Rosebay Willow herb)

Lorraine, aged 8

SEPTEMBER

Cooler air quenches
Oppressive heat,
Where I fly
With swallows
In night's new dreams.

Nostalgia dribbles
From dim stars,
Recalling childhood's
Safe scenes,
And parents' presence

In protective proximity;
When
A stampede of tomorrows
Galloped into hazy realms
Of sunlight -

Dappling my paths
Through golden glades,
Where swift flight
Of exuberance
Heightened joy's hold.

Now, September
Portends an end.
Dusk gathers:
Fears of the unknown
Permeate old dreams

With older consequences,
And experience,
Master of fortune, beckons
Into leaf-strewn autumn's
Whispering domain.

SUMMER SONG

Morning spanned the lawn
with silent shine; I ran
before my years,
under canopies of bird-song,
where blotches of blown blooms
scattered pollen
down my plunging wake:

There, Summer sang
its serried hymns
of swaying grass
in Spring's last tremble,
where, young and free,
I flashed through time's
tree-cast, corn-gold dapples.

It was here I halted,
surprised, and unaware
of retrospective joy -
briefly glimpsed
in spans of sunlight:
Through the crowded years
Of fond recall.

(Runner-up in Norfolk Writer's 'Summer Children' Competition)

Indigo Dreams Publishing
Cookworthy Moor
Halwill
Beaworthy
Devon
EX21 5UU

www.indigodreams.co.uk